BENDING ACADEMY: *FIRE* #1

LIGHT IT UP!

Published by Scholastic Australia in 2026.

Scholastic Australia Pty Limited
PO Box 579 Gosford NSW 2250
ABN 11 000 614 577
www.scholastic.com.au

Part of the Scholastic Group
Sydney · Auckland · New York · Toronto · London · Mexico City · New Delhi
Hong Kong · Buenos Aires · Puerto Rico

ISBN 978-1-76181-071-8

Printed in China.

Scholastic Australia's policy, in association with its printers, is to use papers that are renewable and made efficiently from wood grown in responsibly managed forests, so as to minimise its environment footprint.

BENDING ACADEMY: FIRE #1

LIGHT IT UP!

Written and illustrated by Ash J. Wu

Meet the Team!

Jiyung

Adaki

Chuan

Sujun
Aera
Tearan

Chapter One

Adaki struggled to keep the small fireball burning between his hands. He tried to adjust his stance, but his foot slipped back on the wet floor. **"Gah!"** Adaki yelped. The fireball shrank even more. Adaki groaned in frustration. If he messed up, he knew he wouldn't get to try again . . .

It was a cold, rainy night out on the ocean. In other words, the worst possible conditions for firebending. The weather on Karr Lok Island was often unpredictable, especially after dusk, but it couldn't be helped. After all, fire-fishing was most effective in the dark. The brighter the bender's flames were, the more sardines were lured to the surface of the water. When they jumped to reach the fire, the fishermen would catch them in a giant net. Selling these fish at the local market was how Adaki's family had made their living for generations.

But right now, there were no sardines in sight. The faint flickering of Adaki's fireball was barely illuminating the water.

"Adaki, how is it going back there?" His father Adaro's voice boomed. He and three other fishermen held a giant net over the side of the boat.

Daiki, the oldest fisherman, sighed. "I'm still not seeing any fish. If this goes on for much longer, it'll be sunrise . . ." His gray eyebrows furrowed, deepening his forehead wrinkles.

"I've almost got it, **hold on!"** said Adaki. He concentrated his chi—his life energy—into the fireball. But he was distracted. He had water in his eyes, and his spiky hair tickled his forehead. "Urgh, now even my own hair is working against me!" Adaki grumbled.

Just when he thought things couldn't get any worse, Adaki felt something jump onto his shoulder.

Something furry and damp, with sharp claws . . .

"What the—?!" said Adaki. He turned to see a pair of glowing eyes staring back at him. **"AAAH!"** Adaki stumbled and slipped onto his backside. The small, dull fireball he'd kept alight went out completely.

Adaro hurried over to where Adaki sat on the deck. "What happened?"

"Something attacked me!" said Adaki, looking around. But the creature with the glowing eyes was nowhere to be seen. "Where'd it go?"

Adaki's dad helped him to his feet. "All right, you'd better let me take over."

"I swear I almost had it that time!" said Adaki. "Please let me try again!"

Adaro smiled and patted Adaki on the shoulder. "Sorry, son, that's all for tonight. **You can try again next week.** Sit down and rest."

Adaki sighed. "Fine . . ." As he walked past the fishermen holding the net, he asked, "Hey, can I help you guys with that?"

Hidemaro, another fisherman, looked Adaki up and down. "Maybe when you're older. This net is heavy," he said.

Eizo laughed. "Yeah, **you've still got some growing up to do, little matchstick."**

Despite the cold, Adaki felt his cheeks turn hot with embarrassment. Sure, he was a little small for his age, but matchstick?! That was going too far.

Adaki sighed and slumped on the seat at the back of the boat. From there, he had a clear view of his father.

Adaro stood tall, rolling his wide shoulders and stretching his burly arms. Then he focused and drew in a deep breath. With a few sharp thrusts of his hands in a wide circular motion, he created **a giant fireball.** It was bright enough to illuminate the entire boat.

Adaki's eyes widened. "Wow . . ." He'd seen his dad fire-fish before but was always amazed by his bending skills.

"See how it's done, kid?" Daiki called.

Adaki watched as his dad carefully moved the fireball between his hands to hover it above the water. He had no idea how his dad managed to keep it burning so bright and intensely, even in the wind and rain.

The other three fishermen readied the net.

The water rippled. Silver shapes darted just below the surface . . .

Then suddenly . . .

SPLASH!

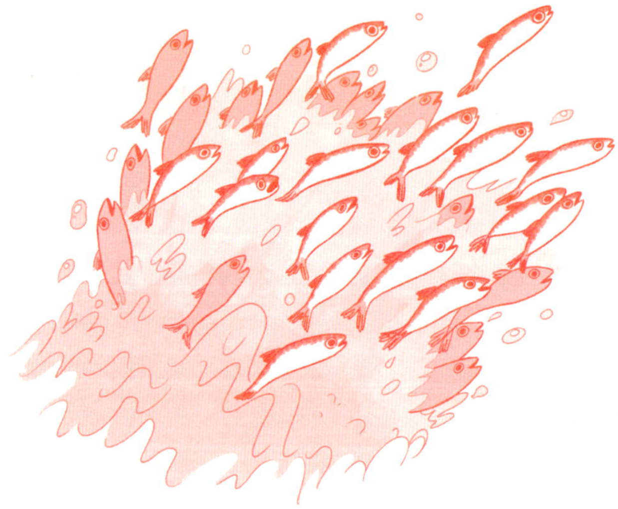

An entire school of silver fish leaped out from the water and up into the air, drawn to the powerful glow. Their scales sparkled in the light of the fire. With a swift unified movement, the three fishermen tossed the net and caught the school of flying fish. They cheered at the giant haul.

"Nice going, Adaro!" called Daiki. **"This is the biggest catch of this week!"**

"At this rate, we might need **a bigger net!"** said Adaro.

"Yeah, and **a bigger boat!"** Eizo chimed in.

"I'll get right on it—when money starts sprouting from fire lily blooms." Adaro laughed.

Adaki grinned. It was amazing seeing the team at work—not to mention his dad's incredible firebending. The fact that he could crack jokes and firebend at the same time was incredible to Adaki.

But . . . Adaki couldn't help but notice that everything seemed to go better when he was out of the way.

Thanks to Adaro's firebending, they quickly caught as many fish as they could carry. Then they returned to shore.

Back home—a stone cottage not far from the beach—Adaki couldn't sleep. He looked to his side.

On his wall was a parchment poster of his heroes, **the Flame Throwers.** They had won the Nationwide Bending Competition four years ago and were **the best Firebenders ever to come from Karr Lok Island.** Adaki had always wanted to be part of an amazing team like them.

But the fact that he couldn't even help his dad with fire-fishing made him question whether his goal was even possible.

Would he ever get the chance to **prove himself** and **live his dream?**

Chapter Two

The next day . . .

"*Psst!* Adaki!" a voice whispered.

Adaki sat up straight. "Huh, wha—?" In a daze, Adaki looked at his friend **Jiyung,** who was sitting next to him. She tilted her head repeatedly toward the front of the classroom, her hair buns bobbing along with the movement.

"Well, Adaki?" The teacher, Sifu Saruzo, stood, tapping her foot. "Instead of **counting koala-sheep,** how about you count your blessings that I'm in a good mood today?"

Counting koala-sheep? Oh no . . . Adaki realized **he must've fallen asleep during meditation class!**

Before he could apologize, the gong rang.

"That's break," said Saruzo. "Use your ten minutes of freedom wisely." She gave Adaki a final glare over her horn-rimmed glasses before leaving the room.

Some of the other students giggled.

Adaki slumped into his seat and rubbed his bloodshot eyes.

Sujun, another one of Adaki's friends, put a hand on his shoulder. Concern filled Sujun's freckled face. "You don't look so well. Have you been eating properly? I've got a bag of sizzle crisps if you want some."

"I didn't sleep well," Adaki explained. "I went fire-fishing with my dad last night."

"On a school night?" Jiyung asked.

"Yeah, we weren't meant to stay out as late as we did, but I messed it up because I couldn't bend the perfect fireball." Adaki sighed. "Plus some **weird bug-eyed creature** landed on my shoulder."

"Bug-eyed creature?" said a curious voice. Their friend **Aera** suddenly popped over Adaki's shoulder.

Adaki jumped in surprise, his cowlick standing on end. "Whoa! A little warning next time, Aera?"

"Sorry." Aera cackled. Her small size made her stealthy—she took advantage of this regularly for her own amusement. A playful grin spread across her face. "My grandma hates when I sneak up on her too. But what was the creature you saw?"

Adaki shrugged. "I dunno. It was creepy, though. Hopefully I'll never see one again . . ."

"Hey, guys!" Tenshin, another kid in their class, burst into the room. **"There's a fight going on in one of the training rooms!"**

The whole class stampeded down the corridor to the fifth-grade training room. Adaki, Jiyung, Sujun, and Aera weaved through the crowd to get a better view.

Two groups were on the **giant stage** in the center of the hall. Each had four members, but the members of one of the teams were clearly older.

The tallest of the older team kept using a **spinning kick attack, creating fire wave**

after fire wave. Another member was rapidly throwing **disc-like fire projectiles.** Their opponents had no choice but to keep dodging, losing chances to attack. Making the battle even tougher, the other two members of the older team were creating **pillars of fire!**

"Whoa, these guys are **amazing!"** said Adaki, his eyes wide and sparkling.

Even Aera looked impressed. "I'll admit, their firebending is really strong . . ."

"Their age gives them an advantage, but they've clearly trained hard to be this good!" said Jiyung rationally.

Sujun nodded. **"They certainly work well together."**

It was no surprise that the older group quickly had the younger one backed into the corner. Soon the older kids had knocked every member of the younger group off the stage.

Once the fight finished, the participants shook hands. The winning group looked smug, whereas the losers were a little embarrassed but smiling regardless.

Then a firebending teacher, **Sifu Chuan,** strode onto the stage. She smiled down at the audience. "Hello, Sunray Academy fifth graders! I hope you enjoyed our demonstration. A round of applause for our talented players!" Her strong, confident voice echoed across the hall.

The crowd clapped but also murmured in confusion.

"Demonstration?" Sujun raised an eyebrow.

"Shhh, let's hear what she has to say!" Adaki

whispered to his friends. **Chuan trained some of the best Firebenders from their village, including members of Adaki's beloved Team Flame Throwers.** She had a reputation for being tough as nails. Nobody had ever **dared** to get on her bad side—out of both respect and fear. So when Chuan asked the crowd to quiet down, everyone immediately went silent.

Chuan crossed her muscular arms. "As I'm sure you know, **the Regional Bending Tournament is in four weeks.** This sign-up sheet has been out since last week." Chuan waved a piece of parchment paper. "I couldn't help but notice we have **no entrants from any students from fifth grade . . ."** The teacher smirked. "So? Did that match inspire you?"

There were more whispers among the audience.

"Is she **seriously** trying to get us to sign up for the Regional Bending Tournament? That would mean we could be up against *sixteen-year-olds*!" whispered Sujun, who had just celebrated their eleventh birthday last week. Adaki's stomach rumbled as he remembered the delicious pandan cake that Sujun's parents—professional chefs—had baked.

"The odds would clearly be against anybody our age . . . That losing team were at least sixth graders and they still got their butts kicked!" said Jiyung, fiddling with her bracelets nervously.

"She's probably just trying to fill spaces," said Aera.

Adaki raised an eyebrow. Was Aera right? Or did Chuan really believe they had a chance against the older kids?

"There are a couple more things to keep in mind," Chuan continued. "Some of you may be interested to know that there is a **prize of one hundred gold pieces for the winning team.** Maybe consider giving back to the school, if you're uncertain of what to spend it on." She winked.

Adaki's eyes widened. One hundred gold pieces was *a lot* of money . . . He remembered last night's conversation between his dad and the other fishermen about getting a bigger boat:

"I'll get right on it—when money starts sprouting from fire lily blooms!"

If Adaki won the gold, he could buy a larger net *and* a larger boat! He sat up straighter at the thought of helping his father.

"Also, **I will personally tutor any fifth grade team that enters!"** said Chuan, her voice booming. "And that's a promise!"

Adaki couldn't believe it. Sifu Chuan usually only taught eighth grade and up! That was the last push he needed. He raised his hand. "I'll do it! I'll enter!"

The entire crowd looked at him and gasped. Even Adaki's friends were surprised.

"Fantastic." Chuan smiled down at them from the stage. "Come to the training hall at the end of the school day. And who will you be entering with?"

Adaki shot a glance at Jiyung, then Sujun, then Aera. **"These guys right here!"**

Adaki's three friends' jaws dropped. "Wait . . . **WHAT?!"**

Chapter Three

After the break, they rushed to math class. To Adaki, it felt like the longest hour and a half of his life. He wanted so badly to talk to his friends more about the tournament. **He had said they'd enter together, but now he needed to convince them to actually do it.**

After what seemed like an eternity, lunchtime came around. Adaki grabbed some rice balls from the canteen and hurried over to his friends' table.

"So? Have you given it any more thought?" asked Adaki.

Jiyung sighed, waving a sheet of calculations.

"What am I looking at?" said Adaki.

"I've run the numbers, and our chances of

winning are low," said Jiyung. "Plus, I *always* mess up under pressure—even math exams! And I'm great at math! If I couldn't handle that, then I don't know how I could face someone in a *firebending* match . . ." Jiyung covered her face in embarrassment.

Though in class she was the first to raise her hand with the correct answer, **Jiyung fell apart as soon as she was nervous.** In the last math exam, Jiyung got so overwhelmed that **she burst into song—**the Fire Nation national anthem—and was unable to stop singing until she was removed from the exam hall. Everyone applauded, but she was deeply embarrassed by the experience.

Adaki could relate—he felt his firebending was much better when he wasn't under the pressure of helping his dad.

"But it would be different! We'd be **fighting together,** so we could give each other confidence!" said Adaki.

"I've heard Sifu Chuan is an incredible firebending teacher," said Sujun. **"The training could be life-changing."**

Adaki grinned. "I agree! Does that mean you'll enter the tournament?"

Sujun's long hair swayed as they shook their head. "Don't count me in just yet. I don't know if it's smart to pick fights we can't win."

"Aw, c'mon! We could so win!" said Adaki. "What do you think, Aera?"

"I think it could be fun." Aera shrugged. "Plus, with one hundred gold pieces, I could treat my grandma to a nice holiday—**maybe even as far as the Earth Kingdom!"** The Earth Kingdom was across the ocean from Karr Lok Island. "They have really cool animals there, like giant badger-moles!"

"Sounds kind of scary . . ." said Sujun with knotted eyebrows.

"The prize money would be split across the four of us . . . so it would be more like twenty-five gold pieces each," Jiyung said under her breath as she did more math.

"Actually," said Sujun, stroking their chin, "with twenty-five gold pieces, **I could get that cast-iron wok I saw at the market the other week . . . and the ingredients for superspicy soufflé . . ."** Superspicy soufflé was a specialty dish of Kirachu Island. Sujun's father had traveled there before Sujun was born and often talked about the incredibly spicy eggy experience of the soufflé. Sujun had always been curious whether the dish really was as good as their father claimed.

"Yeah!" Adaki grinned. "If we won, I'd buy a bigger boat and fishing net for my dad! It would be amazing! And even if we lost—which totally isn't gonna happen—we'd still get training in firebending from one of the great sifus!" Adaki punched the air. "I could be a better fire-fisherman that way!"

Jiyung sighed. "Well . . . I guess we could always see how the training goes. Surely Sifu Chuan wouldn't let us fight in the real thing if she thought we weren't good enough."

"*Yes!*" Adaki said, then stuffed the last rice ball into his mouth and swallowed.

Sujun's eye twitched. "Did you even chew that?"

Adaki stood up. "No time. **I'm gonna go sign us up right now!"** He sprinted to the corridor where the sign-up sheet was hung on the wall. He picked up the nearby brush pen and wrote his name.

Jiyung, Sujun, and Aera caught up to him.

"We can write our own names, Adaki," said Jiyung, putting a hand on his shoulder.

"I was worried you'd change your minds by the time I got here!" admitted Adaki.

One by one, Adaki's friends added their names to the sign-up sheet. He bounced with excitement. "*Woo!* We'll need a team name, right?"

"Well, you're the one who talked us all into this . . . so how about **Team Adaki** for now?" suggested Aera.

"Does that mean I'm the leader?" asked Adaki excitedly.

"No!" said Jiyung, Sujun, and Aera at the same time.

The friends laughed together as the gong rang. Lunchtime was over, but Adaki didn't mind—each passing minute brought the team closer to starting their tournament training!

Chapter Four

Adaki was buzzing with excitement the entire school day. When the final gong rang out, he sprinted to the practice hall, where Chuan would lead **their first training session.**

When Adaki got there, the hall didn't look how he imagined it at all. There was no practice ring set up. No sandbags or dummies with targets to strike. Instead, Chuan was laying out woven **bamboo mats** on the wooden floors. In front of them were **scrolls and ink brush pens.**

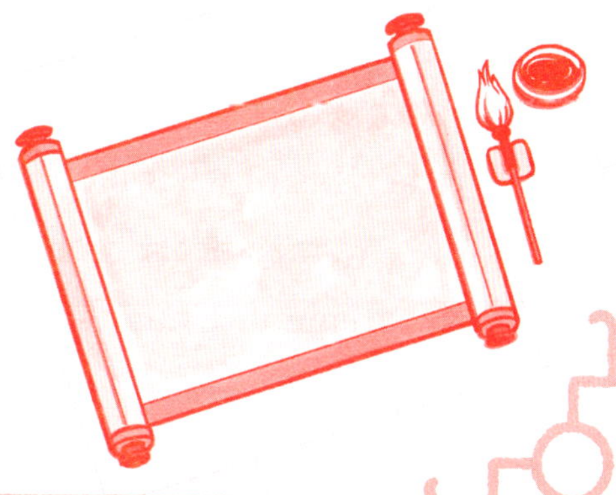

Adaki tilted his head. "What's all this stuff for, Sifu?"

Chuan glanced over at him as she laid the final bamboo mat down. "You're Adaki, right? I'll explain when your friends get here."

One by one, Jiyung, Sujun, and Aera entered the hall. Judging by their expressions, they were excited but weren't sure what to make of the situation either.

Chuan pointed. "Everybody come and sit down on a mat!"

Each kid sat on their own mat. Chuan stood over them, pacing as she spoke. "So, as you all know, this competition involves **a firebending match to be the last team in the ring.** One wrong move or a single moment of hesitation will get you knocked out. On top of that, you have an entire audience watching every second of the match. **Your pride and the honor of your team, your family, and even the reputation of this school will be on the line."** The sifu slowly looked from Adaki, to Jiyung, to Sujun, to Aera—making intense eye contact with each of them. "I assume that in signing up, you accept the risks of what it could mean to fail."

Adaki's heart raced with a mixture of nerves and excitement. Chuan's speech was a little scary, but he was ready for the training to begin. Was Chuan going to teach them some amazing projectile firebending today? Or maybe that spin kick the older kid did in the demonstration? Or maybe they'd learn one of the Flame Throwers' signature moves!

"Now, I'm sure all of you have great respect for **Avatar Szeto**—not only as a hero to our nation, but as an amazing bender as well," said Chuan.

Adaki sat up straighter at the mention of Szeto. The Avatar was the only living person who was able to bend all four elements: **fire, air, water, and earth.** Previous incarnations of the Avatar had come from the Air, Water, and Earth Nations, but Szeto was born into the Fire Nation just like them.

"Our training here today will honor him," said Chuan with a serious expression. Then she clasped her hands together. "On that note . . . **who here likes math?"**

Jiyung raised her hand. No one else did.

"Well, at least one person is going to enjoy our practice," said Chuan with a grin. "Because that's what we'll be doing!"

"*Yay!*" cheered Jiyung.

Adaki **gasped in horror.** "We're doing . . . *math*?!"

Sujun covered their face and groaned. "I regret everything."

Aera jumped to her feet. **"Was this whole thing a trick to get us to do extra math lessons?!"**

Chuan laughed and waved her hand. "No tricks. This is going to help you improve your firebending, I promise!"

Aera slowly sat down, glaring suspiciously.

"Okay, everyone," said Chuan with a smile. "I want you to count to five aloud repeatedly." Chuan tapped the ground lightly with her knuckle. "This is the pace—*one, two, three, four, five. One, two, three, four, five.*"

Adaki tried not to laugh. She wanted them to count to five? If that was as bad as the math lesson was going to get, he was sure he could handle it.

"While you count, I'm going to call out different angles. Forty-five degrees, ninety degrees, one hundred and eighty degrees. It can help to think of them like fractions of a pie. As soon as I call out an angle, you're going to have to draw it as quickly as you can."

Jiyung nodded enthusiastically.

Counting, degrees, pies . . . Adaki felt like his head was spinning!

"We've got this, guys!" said Jiyung, excited to start.

"Woo, go team," said Sujun sarcastically.

Aera yawned.

Jiyung opened her mouth to say something, but Chuan cut her off.

"Okay!" said Chuan. "Shall we begin?"

Everybody grabbed their brush pens.

"Ready, set, go!" said Chuan.

They started counting in unison. "One, two, three, four, five . . . One, two, three, four, five . . ."

Adaki spoke the numbers over and over. Very soon they didn't sound like real words anymore. He started to think about how pointless this felt. Unless the plan was to bore their opponents off the mat in the tournament . . . ?

Suddenly Chuan yelled, "Ninety degrees!"

Adaki, Sujun, and Aera drew the angle, but **Jiyung froze,** shocked by how loud the instruction was. Then she started to draw the ninety-degree angle a few seconds later than her friends.

"One hundred and eighty degrees!" Chuan continued. "Forty-five degrees! Three hundred and sixty!" As the exercise continued, Aera stopped counting, while Jiyung had stopped drawing angles. Sujun kept trying to neaten the scribbly angles they'd drawn but only made them worse.

As he hurried to draw, Adaki lost his rhythm *and* his count. "One, three . . . four, one, three—"

He knocked over the ink pot. **"Ah!"**

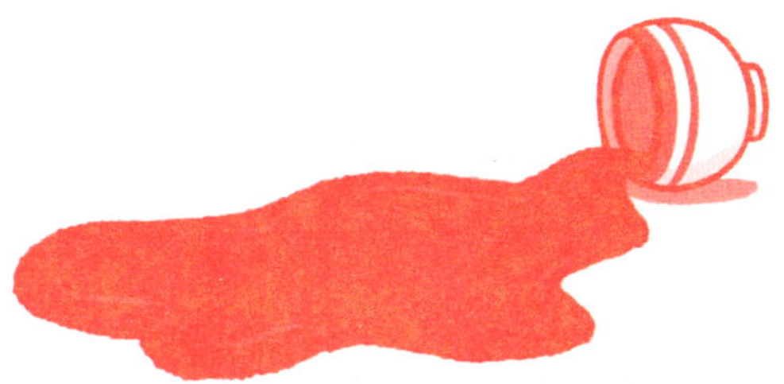

Chuan raised a hand. "All right, that's enough! So where did we go wrong?"

"Adaki knocked over the pot?" said Aera.

"Sujun lost the rhythm," said Adaki.

Sujun leaned over to look at what Jiyung drew. "Jiyung only drew the first angle you said!"

Chuan snapped her fingers. **"Exactly! In fact, you all did poorly! Which is great, because it's what I expected and hoped for!"**

Everyone was speechless. Jiyung looked devastated. “Wait . . . what?”

“I’m not going to make you do that exercise again,” said Chuan. “Because I guarantee the outcome will be the same—everyone will mess up.” Chuan stood up on her mat. “I’m going to pop out for five minutes to water the peace lily in my office. When I get back, I’d like to hear your thoughts on how this training relates to firebending in the tournament.”

Chuan left the room.

There was a brief silence, broken by Aera standing

up. “Well, I’m out. **This is *not* the training I signed up for.”**

“B-but, Aera—” said Jiyung, reaching after her. “I’m sure there’s an explanation for—”

Sujun interrupted. “Yeah, if I knew this was going to be math-related, I never would’ve agreed to it.”

Jiyung frowned. “Shouldn’t we at least wait for Sifu Chuan to—”

“W-wait!” Adaki jumped to his feet. “I know this whole thing seems **really pointless,** but there’s gotta be a reason for it, right?”

Jiyung’s eye twitched. In an attempt to calm down, she took a deep breath in and out. In . . . and out . . .

Adaki continued, “Chuan trained Haru from the Flame Throwers—one of the best Firebenders I’ve ever seen! I hate math as much as you guys . . . but I’m sure if we just do what she says we’ll get to do *actual* firebending soon!”

“That’s ENOUGH!” Jiyung yelled. As she did so, she **breathed out a ball of fire** that launched straight up toward the ceiling!

Chapter Five

The fireball burned out once it hit the stone ceiling, leaving a dark mark. They all stared in shock. No one had ever seen Jiyung do that before.

"Whoa, Jiyung, did you just—" said Adaki.

"Not another word!" Jiyung held up a hand. "I'm sick of hearing you guys bad-mouth math! **Don't you realize Avatar Szeto wouldn't have been able to save our nation without it?"**

They all fell silent at Jiyung's declaration.

Jiyung pointed at Adaki. "During the famine, Szeto helped farmers like your late grandfather!"

Adaki's eyebrows rose. His grandfather was considered a wild rebel within his family for not going into fishing like everybody else. But Adaki had always thought that was pretty cool.

Jiyung then pointed at Sujun. "Without Szeto funding workers like Adaki's grandfather, you wouldn't have the flour for dumplings, or bread, or tons of other recipes!"

Sujun gasped at the thought. "No dumplings . . . ?!"

"Exactly!" Finally, Jiyung turned to Aera. "And your grandma grew up during the famine, right? So if Szeto hadn't helped those farmers, she could've starved!"

Aera grimaced. "Yikes. I never thought of that . . ."

"Exactly!" said Jiyung. She sighed, calming down. "So I'd appreciate if everyone would stop bad-mouthing my favorite subject, all right?"

Sujun scratched their head. "Sorry . . . I'd probably be upset if you all complained about us having to do a cooking project."

"Yeah, sorry . . ." said Aera. "But . . . can I ask how you breathed that **awesome fireball?"**

Jiyung looked up at the ceiling. "Um. I dunno. I was just feeling really passionate about defending math. I guess I took a deep breath beforehand for a few seconds?"

"It was amazing! You were looking straight up,

so your head was **a perfect forty-five degree angle** to your body!" said Adaki.

"Wait . . . What did you say, Adaki?" asked Sujun.

Adaki blinked. "What, that it was amazing? She was looking straight up."

"No, you said it was a forty-five degree angle!" said Jiyung. **"YOU DID MATH,** without even being forced to!" Jiyung's eyes welled with happy tears.

"Oh yeah!" said Adaki. "Wait, I think I'm starting to get why we're doing this!"

Aera stared. "Really?!"

"It looks like I got back at the perfect time!" said Chuan as she walked over to her mat.

"That five minutes went quickly," said Sujun.

"Right, well, to be honest, I went to water my plant, but on my way there I remembered I'd killed it yesterday, so I just came straight back," admitted Chuan. "But it seems like you had a **revelation** while I was away! Care to explain?"

"R . . . Right!" Adaki nodded. "So when you left, we were complaining about the exercise—"

Sujun and Aera looked at each other awkwardly at the inclusion of this detail.

"Very honest of you," said Chuan, crossing her arms. "Go on."

Adaki continued to speak quickly and enthusiastically. "And well, of course the only person who wasn't complaining was Jiyung—and she got annoyed and told us about how Szeto used math to save the Fire Nation and stuff—but just before that, she took this huge breath in and then blew a *giant* fireball at the ceiling!" Adaki pointed upward. Then he panted, having not taken a breath at all during his speech. “And she aimed it at . . . a perfect forty-five-degree angle . . . so the point is . . . strong angles can make your firebending more powerful!”

“Very good!” said Chuan. “Did everyone get that? Jiyung was able to firebend so well because she directed her body into the move—at a precise angle! **Firebending is an extension of the body,** and therefore a stronger form means a stronger move. You want to be precise when you firebend—especially in a tournament, where every second counts and any weak moves could give your opponent the advantage!”

Sujun stroked their chin thoughtfully. “Jiyung took a **deep breath in . . .** Is that why we were counting at the same time as drawing the angles? Because you have to control your breath too?”

Chuan nods. “Right!” She placed a hand on her stomach. “When you inhale, breathe deeply so you feel your belly expand. Then continue inhaling until you feel your lungs expand too. That way, you will have concentrated the chi—the life energy—within yourself, ready to be released as fire as you exhale.”

Chuan took up a solid, wide-legged stance. “And after you do that, you need a strong form to direct that firebending how you want. Whether that's through a punch"—she breathed out and punched a blast of fire, her arm at a perfect right angle to her body—"or a kick!" Chuan took a deep breath, then ran and struck the air with a kick, her leg sweeping parallel to the ground. When she landed, she took a form with her front leg bent and her back leg straight. "Or . . . through your breath itself!" Chuan breathed in, looked directly upward, and breathed a fan of fire into the air.

"Whoa!" said Adaki, staring up at the flames.

When Chuan finished her demonstration, Adaki, Jiyung, Aera, and Sujun clapped.

"Thank you," said Chuan, raising a hand. "But there's one more thing . . . **One final ingredient to being a great Firebender! And that is passion."** She looked at Jiyung. "Your passion for math is what allowed you to firebend so powerfully."

"I guess it did." Jiyung was flattered but a bit embarrassed. "But I still messed up in the exercise."

"The key is to **build confidence** based on your passion. Focus on that rather than how well you are performing. Let your excitement drive your energy. I think you slipped up in the exercise because you were more focused on your nerves, and your friends criticizing something you love."

"That is true," said Jiyung. "All their complaining did get on my nerves."

"I'm sorry!" said Adaki.

"We promise it won't happen again. Especially now that we're starting to get why we should take it more seriously," said Sujun.

"Exactly." Aera nodded. "From now on, we're math defenders too! Especially if it means we won't be on the receiving end of Jiyung's fire breath . . ."

Chuan smiled. "Jiyung, if you firebend and draw from your enthusiasm, you could be one of the strongest Firebenders of your age!"

Jiyung grinned and sat up straighter, looking more confident already.

They wrapped up that first session soon after.

For the rest of the week, the team's training focused on simple firebending attacks using these strong mathematical angles. Chuan coached them through straight and diagonal punches and kicks.

As they reached the end of the first week, Adaki was exhausted. But even at bedtime, he lay awake wondering what they would learn in the weeks to come . . .

Chapter Six

The following Monday, Adaki, Sujun, Jiyung, and Aera were eating lunch together when a group of four older kids approached.

"Hey, isn't that the winning team from the demonstration?" asked Adaki.

Aera looked over at them. "Not these bozos . . ." she muttered under her breath. "They may be good Firebenders, but they're also **total jerks."**

One of the boys stepped forward.

"Hey," he said, "you must be those fifth graders entering the tournament!" His smug grin wrinkled the bandage over his nose.

"That's right," said Adaki. "I'm Adaki, and these are my friends Aera, Jiyung, and Sujun! We're gonna win the tournament!"

One of the girls on their team snickered.

Adaki tilted his head. "What's so funny?"

"Don't worry about it," said the boy, still smirking. "I'm **Tearan,** the laughing girl is Moriko, and that's Akito and Botan. We're entering the competition as well." Tearan brushed off his spiked shoulder pads.

"Neat!" said Adaki. "Who is your mentor?"

"Sifu Joron. You might've heard the rumors that he's descended from the ancient warlords . . . He's all about no mercy—**winning at all costs,** if you catch my drift," said Tearan.

"Yeah, I get it . . ." Adaki smiled and nodded, even though he didn't understand what Tearan meant at all. Sifu Joron only taught the older students.

Akito ran a hand through her wild head of hair. "You may have seen us kicking butt in the demonstration recently. We're only getting better with each training session."

"Modest, aren't we . . ." said Aera under her breath.

Botan nodded in agreement with Akito. The dainty mole on his cheek contrasted with his big size. "I wouldn't want to be whoever has to go against us. There's a reason our name is **Team Undefeated."** He flexed a muscular arm.

Tearan looked at each of Adaki's team members. He squinted at Sujun, then raised his eyebrows. "Wait, your parents own that dumpling restaurant, right? I was there last night!"

Sujun cleared their throat. "Oh, well, thank you for your patronage . . ."

"I was sat right by the kitchen, actually," Tearan continued. "I heard a voice yelling at someone to get out, then you came out of the kitchen with your eyes all watery. What happened in there?"

Sujun's face turned red. "Oh, that!" They laughed nervously. "The chef was chasing a cat-bat and telling them to get out. And then my eyes were watery . . . because I was cutting onions."

Tearan's eyebrows raised. "Is that so? Because now that I think about it, the chef's exact words were 'Sujun, get out, you've exploded the dumplings *again*!' "

"That can't be right," said Jiyung. "Sujun's great at cooking. We've all tried their dumplings, right?"

Adaki nodded. "Yeah, they bring us some once a week!"

"Sounds like a load of hog-monkey chatter if you ask me . . ." said Aera, glaring at Tearan.

"You calling me a liar, little matchstick?" said Tearan.

Moriko giggled. "Maybe the cat-bat was named Sujun too?" She raised her arched eyebrows.

"That must be the explanation," said Tearan with a mocking wink at Sujun.

Aera crossed her arms. "Don't listen to them, guys They trampled my grandma's fire lily garden a few summers ago and lied about it. **I wouldn't take anything they say seriously."**

Moriko tilted her head at Aera, her long pigtails swaying. "And you," she said. "It's good to see that even a shy koala-sheep like you can make friends."

"With someone other than a weird old hag," added Botan. Akito chuckled in the background.

Aera gritted her teeth.

"Stay flaming, kids. See you all in the ring."

Tearan and his friends laughed as they walked away.

"Urgh! What a bunch of weasel-snakes . . ." said Aera.

"Yeah, that was weird," said Jiyung with narrowed eyes. "What were they talking about? Why would they lie about Sujun like that?"

Adaki shrugged. "Don't worry, we'll settle it in the ring!"

Sujun said nothing. They remained silent for the rest of the day. Adaki tried to get Sujun to laugh by making silly faces during lessons—doing his best elephant-koi fish impression, complete with gulps and fin flapping. **But Sujun didn't even crack a smile.**

Meanwhile, Jiyung thought about how focusing on math last week had made her feel confident. Suddenly, **she had an idea** to cheer her friend up! She shared it with Aera, who agreed that it might work. On their way to their last lesson of the day, they found Chuan and discussed it with her . . .

After their last class, Sujun put their history book in their locker before walking to the training hall. Just outside the door, they spotted a small pile of white powder on the floor. It looked almost like . . . **flour?**

Sujun heard muffled excited voices from inside the hall.

"I think Sujun's here!"

"They're gonna love this! Jiyung, your idea was great!"

"Shhh, here they come!"

Sujun pushed open the door . . .

"SURPRISE!" Adaki, Jiyung, and Aera shouted.

There was what looked like an entire kitchen in the training hall!

Chuan adjusted her apron. "All right, is everybody ready? If it wasn't obvious, **in today's training session . . . we're going to be cooking!"**

Sujun turned as white as the flour on the floor outside.

Chapter Seven

Everyone stood in front of their own stovetop, including Chuan. Adaki glanced across at Sujun. He thought his friend would be excited, but they hadn't said anything since entering the training hall.

"Okay," Chuan said, "today we're going to try to **fry these dumplings** as evenly as possible. Now, you may have heard the rumors that I'm a lousy cook. I haven't prepared any meals since I gave the entire staff food poisoning with my homemade noodles."

"How in the world do you mess up *noodles* that badly?" Aera whispered to Jiyung.

Chuan cleared her throat. "But luckily Sujun's parents, the owners of the Dragon Lotus restaurant, kindly supplied the dumplings we'll be searing today!"

Adaki, Aera, and Jiyung grinned at Sujun. Sujun gave a small smile back but still looked pale.

"Allow me to demonstrate the first fry, for those who are new to cooking," said Chuan. She poured something from a ceramic pot into the pan. "First step is a tiny bit of oil. This is going to stop the dumpling from sticking *and* help it cook."

Chuan shifted her feet back and swirled her hand. "And next, of course . . . **the fire!**" She created a small ring of fire under the pan. As she continued to swirl her hand, the fire burned a little brighter. With her free hand, she used chopsticks to place a single dumpling in the pan.

Adaki perked up at the sizzling sound.

"It smells delicious already!" said Jiyung.

Aera sighed. "I already ate and I'm hungry again."

Sujun just stared at the dumpling in the pan.

Over the next few minutes, Chuan carefully kept the fire burning as she rotated the dumpling now and again. Soon she stopped the fire. She picked up the dumpling with her chopstick. "See how it's evenly browned on each side? **Keeping the fire consistent while flipping the dumpling to create an even cook is our goal for today."** She set the dumpling down in a nearby bowl.

"I'd still eat a burned dumpling," said Aera.

Chuan laughed. "That gives me an idea! If you cook the dumpling perfectly, you have my permission to eat it. But if not . . . I'll eat it myself."

Everyone's jaw dropped!

"That's ruthless . . ." said Jiyung. "And maybe slightly dangerous?"

Chuan walked around the room and put a raw dumpling on each student's plate.

Adaki looked down at it. This exercise *sounded* simple enough. But creating and maintaining a specific strength of flame was the exact technique he had trouble with when it came to fire-fishing. Adaki wondered if the whole team was going to think he was **the weak link** if he messed up and the others got the exercise done perfectly.

Chuan held up a sand timer. "You've got five minutes. Everybody get ready!"

Adaki snapped out of his thoughts. He couldn't be left behind!

"And . . ." Chuan flipped the timer. "Go!"

Adaki scrambled for the chopstick. He accidentally tore the dumpling while rushing to pick it up. **"Whoops!"** On a second try he picked up the dumpling and placed it in the pan.

When Adaki glanced to his side, he saw Sujun pouring a dash of oil into their pan.

Suddenly, Adaki thought of his father. Like Adaro, Sujun was an expert who knew what they were doing. They were in their element. **Adaki was determined not to let his friend down.**

Adaki shook his head, trying to focus again, and turned back to his own countertop. Smoke was already starting to rise from his pan. Then he realized—**"Ah, I forgot the oil!"** Adaki grabbed the ceramic bottle of oil and tipped it on top of the dumpling. He didn't anticipate how quickly the oil would pour out, and now the dumpling had a shiny, slimy sheen.

"Oh wait, should I have taken the dumpling out of the pan first?" Adaki muttered under his breath. He glanced at the hourglass timer. The sand was draining away. "No time to think about that!" Adaki took a deep breath in and out and created a small ring of fire like Chuan had done.

Next he grabbed the chopsticks with his free hand and went to pick up the dumpling. But the oil had made it too slippery! It slipped, it skidded, it tumbled around the pan. Holding his breath, Adaki grabbed for it one last time and picked it up . . . from a cold pan! **His fire had gone out.**

"Firebending needs breath, Adaki!" Chuan reminded him. "No worries, you've got one more minute!"

Adaki looked at the soggy, oily, uncooked dumpling in his pan. If he hadn't gotten distracted by his thoughts at the start, he wouldn't have messed up the exercise . . .

He glanced across to Sujun's pan. The dumpling was evenly browned on each side.

Adaki sighed, then smiled weakly. "Aw, Sujun—**yours came out perfectly!"**

Sujun muttered something under their breath.

Adaki blinked. "Sorry?" He leaned over a little more. "I didn't hear that."

"I said **it's not perfect,"** repeated Sujun with gritted teeth.

"What?" Adaki stared at the dumpling. It really did look perfect to him. Was he missing something?

"This side isn't cooked the same as the others." Sujun lifted the dumpling to show Adaki before putting it back down. "No matter what I do, it doesn't match."

"It honestly looks great to me!" said Adaki. Then the fire under Sujun's pan began to burn more intensely. The flames became larger and larger . . .

"You're wrong. No matter how much I try . . ." said Sujun.

The flames grew and towered over the pan. Adaki's eyes widened.

Sujun yelled, **"IT ISN'T GOOD ENOUGH!"**

As they yelled, there was a ***BOOM***—and a giant puff of smoke filled the training hall.

Once the air cleared, everyone turned to Sujun's pan with wide eyes.

There was no dumpling in sight. But there *was* a single burning lump.

". . . What just happened?" asked Aera.

Sujun hung their head. "The dumplings I bring you guys from the restaurant . . . I didn't cook them. **I'm a terrible chef.** Not only that, but I'm a terrible Firebender," they said. "I have no place on your team. I'm sorry for wasting your time . . ."

Sujun ran out of the training hall, the giant doors swinging shut behind them.

Chapter Eight

Adaki, Aera, Jiyung, and Chuan stood around Sujun's pan.

The lump that used to be Sujun's dumpling had stopped burning but was still giving off smoke.

"Does this mean that what that bully Tearan said . . . was true?" said Jiyung. "Sujun really got thrown out of their family kitchen?"

"It's clear **Sujun feels a lot of pressure,"** said Chuan. "Their dumpling looked perfectly good for most of the cooking session, but they seemed to lose confidence toward the end."

"I feel like this is my fault," said Adaki. "It happened just after I said the dumpling looked perfect . . ." Adaki thought about his embarrassment over not being as good a fire-fisher as his father. Did Sujun feel the same way?

"Why don't you go and talk to them? It might encourage Sujun to open up," suggested Chuan. "The rest of us can be on cleanup duty."

Adaki headed out of the training hall to look for Sujun. Eventually, he found his friend sitting on a bench outside. "Sujun, I'm sorry for what I said . . . about the dumpling being perfect."

Sujun sighed, kicking a nearby stone. "It's okay. I know you were just trying to be nice."

"It can be hard, though, right? To feel like you have to be perfect," said Adaki. "And frustrating to not feel good enough. I think I kind of get it."

"You do?" asked Sujun. "But you always seem so . . . relaxed."

"You should see me when I'm out fire-fishing with my dad!" said Adaki. "It's so embarrassing. I can't firebend anywhere near as well as he can. He's given me so many chances to get better at luring the fish with a fireball, but it's like . . ." Adaki crossed his arms. **"I want to do such a good job that sometimes it stops me from doing a good job.** If that makes any sense . . ."

"It does." Sujun nodded. "That's exactly how I feel too."

"For what it's worth," said Adaki, "Jiyung, Aera, and I aren't friends with you just because you're a chef or whatever. It's because we have fun hanging out with you. And I feel the same way about you being on our tournament team. I don't think we have to be perfect, but . . . we just have to put our strengths together and have fun. I think that's what matters, really."

"I thought you wanted that boat for your dad?" said Sujun.

"Of course, I still do!" said Adaki. "But . . . more than that, **I want to be part of an amazing team with my friends!"**

Sujun smiled and stood up. “Let’s go back in there.”

“Are you sure?” said Adaki.

“Yeah,” said Sujun. “What you said was right. I mean, I don’t judge you for not being a perfect fire-fisherman. So I shouldn’t put so much pressure on myself to be a perfect chef. After all, even in a restaurant, you’re working with other chefs, so you can combine your strengths.” Then they paused, their eyebrows furrowing in thought. “Hold on . . .”

Adaki tilted his head in curiosity. “What is it?”

“I just thought of something,” said Sujun.

Adaki and Sujun headed back to the training hall.

“Good timing. We’ve just finished the cleanup!” said Chuan.

“I’m sorry about that . . .” Sujun bowed. “Thank you for cleaning up. I had to step out of the room to calm down. Talking to Adaki helped.”

“I’m glad!” said Chuan. “Looking out for each other is an important part of team building.”

“Speaking of,” said Sujun. “If this is training for the tournament, wouldn’t it make sense if we all tried to cook the dumpling together? Since we won't be working alone."

Chuan smiled. **"That's an excellent idea!"**

"Yeah, that sounds fun!" said Jiyung.

Adaki cheered. "Let's do it!"

They gathered around Sujun's workstation to cook the last dumpling—and the largest of the batch. Adaki was in charge of the oil, Sujun would do the firebending, Jiyung would keep track of the timing, and Aera grabbed the chopsticks.

"All right," said Chuan. "Three, two, one, go!" She flipped the sand timer once again.

With Sujun's coaching, everybody played their role perfectly. They advised Adaki on how to pour the oil slowly, reminded Jiyung to announce how much time was left every so often, and told Aera when to flip the dumpling. Although Sujun helped them pay extra attention to their duties, everyone made sure to encourage each other throughout.

"And . . . time!" said Chuan.

Sujun quickly stopped firebending. Aera set the chopsticks down.

Chuan walked over, her chopsticks in hand. "All right, let's check this out!"

The kids held their breath as their teacher slowly picked up the dumpling, turning to block their view.

Chuan shook her head. "Oh dear . . ."

"We didn't get to check the final side . . . But I suppose the important thing is that I didn't explode anything this time!" said Sujun.

Adaki grinned. "I'd definitely say that's a positive!"

Chuan turned around. "It really is a shame."

She showed them the dumpling. It was cooked to a golden brown on every side. "This isn't burned or undercooked in the slightest. That means I won't get to eat it!"

Jiyung gasped. "We did it?!"

Adaki punched the air and cheered. **"WOOHOO!"**

"FINALLY we get to eat one!" said Aera.

Sujun was stunned, but then a big smile spread across their face.

Using a knife, Chuan cut the dumpling into four

equal pieces and handed them to the students on plates. "I'd say you've more than earned this reward!"

The kids dove into their dumpling pieces.

"This is definitely the best dumpling I've ever tasted!" said Adaki. "And I've tasted *a lot*."

"This *IS* the perfect dumpling," said Sujun, nodding with confidence.

Once they finished, they all tidied up the training hall together.

Chapter Nine

For the rest of the week, Chuan had Adaki and his friends focused on multitasking. They had to run laps, play catch, and jump over fire-whips, all while firebending!

That weekend, Team Adaki met up on the beach to relax. They played **kuai ball,** a sport that involved keeping a ball up in the air without using their hands. When they grew tired, they sat and watched the ocean. The sun was setting, and the waves were twinkling in the light.

"You know, I really feel like we're gonna win this tournament," said Adaki. "And once we do that, it'll be like anything is possible. We could become

the nation's champions! Plus, I'm sure I'd be good enough to help my dad fish too!"

"If we keep winning the tournaments, that means more prize money, right? Maybe I could even open my own restaurant someday," said Sujun.

"As grand champions, do you think we'd get to meet Avatar Szeto?" asked Jiyung. "That would be **amazing!"**

"You'd definitely have enough money to travel to the Fire Nation capital," said Aera. "I'd rather go to the Earth Kingdom, though. I'd bring my grandma and . . ." She paused. "Another friend."

"Oh, do you mean one of us?" asked Jiyung.

Aera awkwardly scratched her head. "Uh, no . . . I mean . . ." She fell silent. "I don't think I've ever mentioned this **other friend,** though he's been . . . around. We met before I was friends with you guys."

"Whoever he is, we'd love to meet him!" said Adaki.

"Okay . . ." Aera said after a long pause. "But you have to **promise me** not to lose your gourd. Let me just go and get him." She walked up the beach.

Her friends watched her, full of curiosity.

"Do you guys have any idea who she could be talking about?" asked Jiyung.

"No idea . . ." said Sujun. "I've never seen Aera hang out with anybody other than us."

"Whoa, look!" Adaki pointed at Aera.

Aera was several feet away now. With a fluid motion of her shorter arm, **she created what looked like a ribbon of fire.** She moved it through the air in front of her, in the shape of a figure eight. The ribbon floated out over the ocean, spinning and twirling in all sorts of interesting ways.

Adaki's eyes widened. **He'd never seen anything like it before.** With its smooth, flowing spins, it looked more like a waterbending move. "She's firebending?"

"Maybe it's a **special signal** to this friend," said Jiyung. "Like she's asking for him to come here."

Sujun looked around. "I don't see anybody making their way over, though . . ."

Adaki spotted a creature in the distance, flying over the water. "Hey, what is that?"

Sujun stroked their chin. "Is it some kind of bird?"

The dancing fire ribbon caught the attention of the creature. It flew closer to the shore.

“Wait, is that . . . **a cat-bat?”** said Jiyung.

Sujun hid behind Jiyung and Adaki. “Oh no, they really freak me out!”

The eyes glowed, the fur bristled . . . Adaki gasped. “That’s what jumped on me in my dad’s boat. They have **really sharp claws!”** he said.

“And it’s headed toward Aera—we’d better warn her!” said Sujun.

Jiyung waved her arms. **"Aera, watch out!** A *cat-bat*! It might hurt you!"

Aera immediately stopped bending and spun around.

As Adaki, Sujun, and Jiyung ran over to her, the cat-bat turned and flew away.

"Phew, that was close . . ." said Sujun. "Are you okay, Aera?"

Aera didn't make eye contact but nodded.

"That fire ribbon move is so cool! You should teach it to us in the next practice," said Adaki.

"Sorry the cat-bat interrupted what you were doing. Is that friend of yours still coming?" asked Jiyung.

"No . . . I signaled to him, but I guess he was busy," said Aera. "Anyway, I have to go. Later." Aera abruptly turned and headed back up the beach.

"Oh, uh, bye!" Adaki waved. "See you next week!"

"That was sudden," said Jiyung.

Sujun rubbed their chin. "She's probably disappointed that her friend didn't show up . . ."

After school the following week, the kids returned to the training hall. They were surprised to see that **the tournament stage was already set up.**

"Hey, everyone!" Chuan said. "I've just come from a meeting with Headmaster Shion and have some **exciting news!"**

The team perked up.

"One of the advisers to Fire Lord Yosor, Kazu Mori, will be visiting our school next week. We've decided to **shift the tournament a week earlier** so that he can attend!" said Chuan.

Everyone's jaw dropped.

"B-but wait, doesn't that mean—" Sujun stammered.

Jiyung finished their sentence, her eyes wide. **"We're losing a week of training!"**

Chapter Ten

After Chuan delivered the shocking news, it took a while for Jiyung, Sujun, and Aera to settle down. The only optimist was Adaki.

"Come on! If Sifu thought we weren't ready for the tournament, she would've said something by now!" said Adaki.

"That's right," said Chuan. "We only have two final areas to cover: **stage control and capture the lantern."**

"Is one week enough time to learn both of those things?" asked Aera.

"Sure!" said Chuan. "You've already mastered the fundamentals of firebending, improved your confidence, problem solved as a team, *and* learned to

firebend while multitasking. These final topics will be a piece of cake!"

For the first half of the week, they focused on stage control, which meant **using moves that pushed their opponents back and out of the ring.** Just as Chuan had predicted, their previous training helped them to learn quickly. She taught them some new techniques that would be useful in the tournament: **fire waves, low and high fire vortex kicks, and fire pillars.** Sujun was particularly good at vortex kicks, since they'd practiced making a ring of fire for cooking.

Since their opponents would also use these moves, the team split into pairs to practice both attacking and defending. During their final stage control session, everyone knocked someone else off the stage except Adaki.

Sujun patted Adaki's shoulder after their fight. "I'm sure you'll be able to do it in the tournament," they said.

Adaki forced a smile. "Y-yeah, totally!"

"Could you **modify your fire-fishing technique** to use during a match?" suggested Jiyung.

"Yeah, if you pushed a giant fireball around the stage, that could definitely knock people off!" said Sujun.

Adaki went to speak but paused. He wasn't sure how he felt about relying on his fireball in the tournament since it was always so weak. "Maybe . . . I'll think about it!" He fidgeted with his sleeve.

Halfway through the week, the friends came into the training hall to see a **paper lantern** hanging from a rope on the ceiling.

"Woohoo, capture the lantern!" cheered Adaki.

"It sure is high," muttered Aera, staring at the rope.

"It's times like this I wish I was an Airbender . . . they could just glide up there," sighed Jiyung.

"Most teams focus on winning a bending match by knocking out all their opponents," Chuan said. **"But capturing the lantern that hangs above the ring each round ensures an instant victory.** Obviously it's much harder than it sounds."

"You've got to cut the rope with firebending without setting the paper lantern on fire . . . right?" Sujun said, still squinting up. "But how will the fire not spread to the lantern?"

"Well, the bigger the fire, the faster it burns. You have to **control your bending** to create a fire that's strong enough to cut the rope, but not so strong that it burns and destroys the lantern," explained Chuan.

Jiyung nodded. ***"Balance the scale to create harmony,"*** she said, quoting Avatar Szeto.

Adaki looked up at where the paper lantern hung from the ceiling. He thought about their time at the beach last weekend and realized he'd seen the perfect move to cut the ribbon there. "Hey, remember that ribbon firebending Aera did? That could work well here!"

"Ribbon firebending?" asked Chuan. "That sounds interesting. Do you want to demonstrate?"

Aera froze. After a few moments she shook her head.

"But it's so cool! Please, Aera!" Adaki pouted.

Aera kept shaking her head.

"I think Adaki's right—it could work really well for this," said Sujun. "I don't know if any of us have seen firebending quite like it."

Jiyung nodded. "The control and precision of it is really incredible."

Chuan rubbed her chin. "I must admit, I am curious about this technique of yours, Aera."

"Come on, Aera . . . for the team?" Adaki pleaded with wide eyes.

Aera stared at the ground.

Chuan tilted her head to one side. "Aera, is this something I can help with? Something you might want to discuss in private?"

"I don't know what difference it would make, but . . . fine." Aera shrugged.

Chuan and Aera headed to the far corner of the hall, where they had a whispered conversation.

Aera was shaking her head a lot, but eventually, Chuan seemed to say something that got through to her. The girl sighed and gave a small, hesitant nod.

Then Aera left the training hall. Chuan walked back over to Adaki, Jiyung, and Sujun.

"Where's Aera going?" Sujun asked.

"How do I put this?" said Chuan, scratching her head. **"She's gone to get her friend—**the one who inspired the ribbon technique!"

"How exciting!" said Jiyung.

Soon the door opened slowly. Aera poked her head through. "Sifu Chuan . . . are you sure about this?"

Chuan nodded. "One hundred percent! Come on in!"

Adaki, Sujun, and Jiyung gasped as Aera walked into the room . . . **with a cat-bat on her shoulder!**

Chapter Eleven

"So the cat-bat that showed up on the beach . . . that was the friend you were talking about?" asked Adaki, his jaw agape.

"His name is **Buddy,"** said Aera, petting the cat-bat.

Sujun hid behind Jiyung and Adaki. "Please don't come closer!"

"It might bite you, Aera!" Jiyung's eyes were wide.

Aera's eyebrows furrowed.

Chuan raised her hands. "You're all going to have to **keep an open mind** here. Aera is leading this session now, and this is important to her."

"You agreed to this, Sifu Chuan?!" asked Sujun.

"*She's* the one who suggested it!" said Aera.

"Aera told me about what happened at the beach," said Chuan. "She told me how hurt she was about the way you reacted to her friend. **I wanted to give her a chance to express herself and also for Aera to give you a chance to change your minds."**

Adaki's heart sank. He hadn't picked up on how upset Aera was.

Sujun gulped nervously. "Was there a way to do this without actually bringing the thing in here?"

"You can stay back if you like," Chuan said, "but I'm sure as Aera's friend you want to hear her out."

"Of—of course we do . . ." said Jiyung.

Adaki nodded rapidly.

Aera sighed heavily. "Fine. I know he might just seem like some stray animal to you, **but Buddy is so much more than that.** He was the **only friend** I had when I was younger. You wouldn't believe how loyal a cat-bat can be," she said.

"Wh-what do you mean?" asked Jiyung, confused.

"It's . . . loyal?" asked Sujun. They were still hiding behind Jiyung and Adaki.

Aera nodded. "One time those Team Undefeated bullies followed me home, saying mean stuff. They used to pick on me because I firebend differently." Aera rubbed her left arm, which stopped at the elbow. "But **Buddy swooped in and scared them off.** He almost got hurt, but he did it to protect me." She wiped her eyes, a little teary. "Nobody had defended me before."

Adaki had never seen Aera cry. He felt tears welling in his own eyes.

Aera looked down at the ground. "I never mentioned him to you guys because I was worried you would react badly, and I was right. But **Chuan convinced me to give you a chance** to learn from Buddy too."

Jiyung sighed. "Aera, I'm really sorry. How can we make it up to you?"

"I guess . . . It's like Sifu Chuan said: Keep an open mind," said Aera.

Adaki looked at Buddy. This creature, who was currently licking his own leg, was Aera's first real friend. "I'm sorry too. I only knew them as pests that would steal fish. But **I'd love to try to see what you see!"**

Sujun peered from behind Adaki and Jiyung. “This is gonna be hard for me, but I’ll try my best!” They came out from hiding. “I want to make it up to you too, Aera.”

"That's the spirit!" Chuan smiled approvingly. "So, Aera—*and* Buddy—begin when you are ready!"

Aera put Buddy down the floor. The cat-bat wound around her legs, purring.

"When I was younger, my grandma was my first firebending sifu. We used to practice on the beach." Aera smiled at the memory. "But most traditional techniques involve both arms, so **I struggled to find my balance with some of the forms.** I focused on leg-based techniques for a long time, because whenever I tried to use my shorter arm, I'd mess up. Those bullies would watch and laugh, which only made it worse."

Jiyung shook her head. "Those Team Undefeated meatheads . . ."

"But I'd practice bending with my left arm at night. At first, this was all I could manage." Aera changed her stance, focused, and began to firebend with her shorter arm, creating a delicate ribbon of fire. **"For weeks I practiced after every sunset** but never got better. That is, until . . ."

Aera's ribbon caught the attention of Buddy the

cat-bat. His eyes turned big and dark, and he chased after it.

". . . Buddy showed up," said Aera.

"Wow, look at him go!" Jiyung gasped.

"What incredible determination!" Chuan said. **"He's just like me when the mochi cart goes by."**

Aera chuckled. "His reaction to the ribbon made me laugh so much. **I stopped being self-conscious** and focused on playing with him every evening." She made the ribbon twirl in the air. Buddy spiraled midflight in the same way. "Over time, I could make the ribbon longer and longer, and make it dance more and more. Thanks to Buddy, my firebending has only improved!" Aera pointed her shorter arm upward, and the fire ribbon rocketed toward the ceiling and thrashed the air like a whip.

"Whoa, that's so cool!" said Adaki.

Then Aera slowed the ribbon to a crawl. Buddy's eyes glazed over. He stopped chasing it. He landed on the ground and stared out the window at a passing cicada beetle.

"Ah, interesting!" said Chuan, stroking her chin. "Buddy only reacts when the fire moves in an **unpredictable way.** Likewise, making the ribbon hard to follow will be great for keeping your opponents on their toes!"

Aera nodded. "So the key for this lesson is to firebend the ribbon in a way that gets Buddy's attention. Who wants to try first?"

Jiyung's hand shot up. She created the fire ribbon with no issues but moved the ribbon in straight, predictable lines only. Buddy watched the ribbon for a few moments, but then yawned. Jiyung pouted. "Aw, maybe he just doesn't like me."

"I'll try next!" Adaki stepped forward. He carefully created the fire ribbon. The shape was correct, but it didn't burn bright enough to catch Buddy's attention.

Instead the cat-bat curled in a ball, preparing for a nap. "Darn . . ." Adaki hung his head in frustration.

Finally, it was Sujun's turn. Although they did a good job creating a fire ribbon, their ribbon's dance was slow. Anytime Buddy looked over, Sujun made the ribbon move even slower. Also, Sujun was standing at the opposite end of the hall from Buddy.

"Okay, I think that's enough, Sujun!" called Chuan.

"WHAT?" Sujun shouted.

"Just come over here!" said Aera.

"WHAT?" shouted Sujun again.

Aera rolled her eyes, then walked to the other side of the room to bring Sujun back.

Adaki, Jiyung, and Sujun lined up, eagerly awaiting Aera's feedback.

"So how did we do?" asked Jiyung, wringing her hands.

Aera pointed at Jiyung. "Your ribbon was **too predictable and boring."** Then to Sujun: "Your ribbon was **too slow.** Also . . . you're standing way **too far away."** Then finally to Adaki: "And your ribbon was **too dull."**

Adaki groaned in frustration.

"I'll show you again," said Aera. "Watch carefully."

Aera directed the ribbon with motions of her hand, making it **dance through the air.** The cat-bat jumped and flew after it, trying to swat it. As the ribbon twirled and spun, so did Buddy.

Jiyung watched in amazement. "Wow, I can barely follow the ribbon with my eyes, it's moving so fast!"

"Any opposing team would struggle to keep up with this!" said Chuan.

Aera smiled. She made the ribbon swirl back down to the ground and disappear. Buddy looked around, then meowed grumpily.

"All right, give it another try!" said Aera.

Jiyung created a ribbon, and this time, she made it zigzag in every direction. Buddy flew and spun after it enthusiastically. Jiyung cheered in delight. "I did it!"

Adaki went next. *I WILL play with this cat-bat*, he thought, moving into the proper bending form. Then he created the fire ribbon, which was dim at first. But Adaki wasn't discouraged. He remembered to focus on his breathing, and soon the ribbon became brighter. Buddy looked over with wide eyes, and Adaki knew it was time. He moved the ribbon into the air and made it spin and dance with all of his focus. Buddy launched himself after it. "I did it!" said Adaki.

The others cheered for him.

"Nice going, Adaki! **How about you try hitting the lantern rope?"** suggested Chuan.

Adaki nodded. "Right!" He directed the fire ribbon to slice across the rope. A few moments later, the paper lantern fell. The rope trailed behind it, slowly being eaten by embers.

"I've got it!" said Aera. She used a fire spin move to launch herself higher to catch the lantern. **But the lit rope had also caught Buddy's attention.** He zoomed after it . . . heading **straight toward the flames** of Aera's fire spin!

"Oh no, watch out!" cried Sujun. They **leaped forward** and batted away the fire, saving Buddy from the flames!

Adaki, Jiyung, and Chuan gasped.

Aera, now holding the lantern, landed on the ground. She looked over her shoulder. "What just happened?"

“Buddy flew toward the flames, but Sujun protected him!” said Adaki.

Buddy was winding around Sujun’s legs and purring. Sujun was frozen in shock, staring down at the cat-bat.

"No way!" said Aera. **"That's amazing, Sujun!"**

"I—I'm glad he's okay . . ." said Sujun. Cautiously, they reached down to pat Buddy on the head. But after a few more seconds, they ran to the other side of the hall. "I think that's my cat-bat limit for today!"

Everyone laughed.

"What incredible progress," said Chuan. "From all of you!" She sniffed. Suddenly, tears started streaming down her face. She turned away.

"Are you okay, Sifu Chuan?" asked Jiyung.

"I get it, we've come really far . . ." said Adaki.

"It's true, but that's not why I'm crying . . . **I'm actually super allergic to cat-bats."** Chuan slowly turned around. Her eyes were red, but there was a big grin on her swollen face.

"WHY DIDN'T YOU SAY SOMETHING SOONER?!" cried Aera. She hurriedly rushed Buddy back outside. Chuan sneezed loudly, the sound echoing across the hall.

Thankfully, their sifu quickly recovered. After everyone celebrated learning the new ribbon technique, they practiced it again and again for the final few days of training. Over the weekend, the kids continue to train together on the beach, reviewing every technique they'd learned. Even though they were the youngest competitors, **Team Adaki was starting to think that together, they stood a chance of winning!**

And before they knew it, the day of the tournament had arrived . . .

Chapter Twelve

The academy's competition hall was full of spectators. Adaki, Jiyung, Aera, and Sujun sat on the sidelines, taking it all in.

Adaki was so excited, he had barely slept the night before, and now he felt like he was dreaming. "I can't see a single empty seat!"

"Me neither. I knew it would be busy here, but this is something else," said Jiyung.

Aera nodded. **"I've never seen so many people in one place before."**

"Look, that must be the Fire Lord's adviser!" Sujun pointed. Adviser Kazu stood up. His hair was pulled back into a tight bun, and his thick eyebrows made him look concerned even while smiling.

He was followed by Headmaster Shion and Sifu Chuan. The headmaster was dressed elegantly in black and red formal robes. In contrast, Chuan wore her usual sleeveless training outfit, looking ready for action.

The headmaster cleared her throat, and the audience quieted down.

"Thank you for being here today, for our **fourth annual Regional Bending Tournament!"** said Headmaster Shion. "This beloved competition brings together young Firebenders from around the region for some friendly competition, and to learn from one another. And of course, the winners will move on to the national, and maybe even the worldwide competition! As you know, our special guest, Adviser Kazu Mori, is also here. I speak on behalf of the entire group when I say that it is a great honor to have you here today."

The headmaster bowed to Kazu, who smiled and said, "It is a great pleasure to be here, and an even greater pleasure to be able to see firsthand the incredible bending talent we have in this region. Headmaster Shion has given me the honor of revealing the team matchups for round one. Without further ado . . ."

He took out an envelope from his pocket and opened it. "First up we have . . . **Team Flicker versus Team Adaki!"**

Adaki gasped. "We're up *first*?"

Adviser Kazu, Sifu Chuan, and Headmaster Shion moved into sideline seats as Team Adaki and Team Flicker headed to opposite ends of the stage.

Sujun sighed in relief as they looked at the other team. "I'm glad they're not much older than us."

Adaki noticed Team Flicker were all trembling. "Wow, they look nervous."

Jiyung took deep breaths to calm her nerves. "I won't let myself get in the same state."

"I'm imagining the whole crowd is full of cat-bats," said Aera quietly.

Adaki grinned. "Don't worry. I'm sure we've got this!"

"Let the tournament . . . begin!" Adviser Kazu struck the giant gong.

"All right, like we practiced!" said Jiyung.

Team Adaki ran to the center of the stage. They focused on bending fire pillars and waves to keep their opponents pushed back.

One member of Team Flicker slipped through and ran toward Jiyung, kicking wildly at close range. His attacks weren't extremely powerful, but he was fast. Jiyung was caught off guard! But then she fell back and created space between them. Her opponent grinned, thinking that he'd pushed her into the corner . . .

Suddenly, Jiyung inhaled deeply, assumed a strong stance, and blew her fire breath at him.

"AAIEE!" The Team Flicker member yelled in surprise and backed away so quickly that he fell off the stage.

"OUT!" declared a referee, waving a flag.

Adaki glanced over to see the last of Jiyung's fire breath. "Nice one, Jiyung!"

Since he was distracted by Jiyung's bending, Adaki's next fire wave wasn't as high as the previous ones. One opponent leaped over it and ran toward Adaki with a fiery fist raised.

Just in time, Sujun leaped to defend Adaki with **a fire spinning kick!**

The opponent stumbled back. Sujun continued their fire kicks while moving toward the other Firebender. Their opponent was so focused on trying to land a punch, they didn't realize how close they were to the back of the stage . . .

Sujun did a final spinning attack that threw the Team Flicker member off balance and knocked her out of the ring.

A referee held up a flag. **"OUT!"**

"I need to knock someone out of the ring before this is over!" Adaki said to himself, hoping he'd be able to pull off something as cool as his teammates. He wondered if his dad was watching. Adaki looked at the crowd and spotted him, along with his fire-fishing buddies.

Memories of his last fire-fishing trip filled his mind. Adaki really wanted to make his dad proud today. But while he was distracted, one of the remaining opponents dashed at him.

"ADAKI!" said Sujun, too far away to defend him a second time.

But it was too late. In a moment of desperation, the Team Flicker member tackled Adaki offstage.

Adaki stared in shock at his opponent. "What just happened . . . ?"

"Oops!" said the other boy, noticing he too was outside the ring. **"I panicked!"**

The referee stood over them both. **"OUT!"**

Back onstage, Aera and Jiyung had the final opponent cornered. Aera leaped forward and created a giant fire wave, knocking out the last Team Flicker member.

The referee gave the final shout: **"OUT!"**

Headmaster Shion hit the gong. **"And the team moving on to the next round is . . . TEAM ADAKI!"**

Chapter Thirteen

The crowd cheered. As Adaki rose to his feet, Jiyung, Aera, and Sujun were celebrating onstage. Adaki knew it was amazing that they'd won. So why didn't he feel like cheering?

Headmaster Shion stood up in the stands and announced the next match-up: Team Undefeated vs. Team Candlewicks.

A heavy hand slammed onto Adaki's shoulder, making him spin around. Tearan loomed over him, grinning. "Thanks for the preshow entertainment."

Adaki raised an eyebrow. "Uh, you're welcome . . . ?"

"The rest of your team is actually pretty talented." Tearan grinned. **"Makes things easier for the rest of us to know who the weakest link is."**

The older boy walked away. **Adaki's heart sank.** Tearan was right. Adaki didn't feel like he had contributed to the match at all. If anything, he felt like he'd held the team back.

Team Undefeated and Team Candlewicks made their way onstage. Jiyung, Aera, and Sujun waved at Adaki to join them in the audience. But Adaki couldn't bring himself to sit with them. How could he share in the victory when he had played no part in it?

Instead, Adaki left the arena. He headed back through the school and into the training hall.

Adaki began practicing his bending forms, kicking and punching the air. After half an hour or so, the doors swung open. It was the rest of Team Adaki.

"There you are!" said Jiyung. "We thought you went to watch the other matches with your dad, then realized you'd left completely."

"Just a sec . . ." Adaki was trying so hard to focus on his training. His concentration only fully broke when Aera stepped in front of him.

"We thought you'd want to celebrate our win together," said Aera, frowning.

Adaki couldn't bring himself to look at his friends. "That's the thing . . . it wasn't *our* win. I didn't help at all! Tearan called me the weakest link, and he was right." He kept punching the air with fire jabs.

"That's not true. We all contributed!" said Sujun.

"Tearan just wanted to mess with you," said Aera.

"But I didn't knock anybody out of the ring—and I'm the only one who *got* knocked out," said Adaki. "I let my guard down and lost my focus, as usual . . ." Adaki sank to the floor. He sat cross-legged and rested his chin on his hands.

Jiyung stepped forward. "But, Adaki . . . **if it wasn't for you getting the team together, we wouldn't even be here."**

Sujun nodded. "You believing in the team in the first place made *me* believe in us."

"Exactly, and so what if you lose focus sometimes?" asked Aera. **"I bet you learned way more and practiced way harder than anybody else in our tournament!** And honestly, I don't think *I* would have practiced that much if you hadn't been so excited about it."

"You rose to every weird and random challenge Sifu Chuan threw our way, even if it's not how you pictured training for this tournament!" said Jiyung.

The door creaked open, and Chuan peered around the side. "Jiyung is right."

Jiyung blushed. "Uh, I meant weird and random as a good thing . . ."

Chuan flashed a bright smile. "That's exactly

how I took it." She strode over to Adaki. "Adaki, you adapted to every strange and tricky training session I put you through—all of which were outside your comfort zone. And by the end of each of them, you excelled. That takes flexibility *and* creativity."

Adaki stared up at her, his eyes twinkling in the light. He looked around at his sifu and his friends. "You guys really think so?"

Chuan placed her hand on Adaki's shoulder. "Don't underestimate yourself. Focus on rising to each new challenge, like you did in our training sessions! So long as you keep an open mind, you'll have nothing to worry about."

Chuan offered her hand to Adaki. He took it, and Chuan helped him up to his feet.

"From my perspective," Chuan added, "you are all more than capable of winning this tournament!"

"You're right . . ." said Adaki. He grinned. **"I'm all fired up now!"**

The four friends put their hands together. Adaki looked at the others, his eyes blazing with determination. "Let's get back out there!"

"Yeah!" Sujun, Aera, and Jiyung cheered.

Chapter Fourteen

When they returned to the stadium, the first round was over and Team Adaki was the last fight of the new round, this time against Team Leftovers. However, as Team Adaki waited onstage, there was no sign of the other team.

"What's going on?" said Sujun, looking around.

"Did they get cold feet?"

Suddenly, a student hurried to where Sifu Chuan, Headmaster Shion, and Adviser Kazu sat. She leaned over and whispered to them.

Headmaster Shion nodded, then stood up and announced, "Unfortunately, **Team Leftovers has to drop out due to food poisoning."** She sighed. "That's the last time we serve day-old spicy mudfish and sea prune stew at the canteen . . ."

"We should've warned them not to eat that," whispered Jiyung.

"Who approved that recipe?! My stomach hurts just thinking about it." Sujun groaned.

Headmaster Shion continued, "This forfeit leaves Team Adaki without a team to face in this semifinal bracket. **Therefore Team Adaki is victorious by default and will go through to the finals.** We can commence our championship match: **Team Adaki versus Team Undefeated!"**

Adaki gasped. "Whoa . . ."

From the stands, Tearan and his teammates—Moriko, Akito, and Botan—stood. They confidently strutted onto the stage.

"This is it . . ." said Sujun nervously.

Jiyung whispered to Adaki. "You weren't there for their last matches. **They were super aggressive and won so fast!** If we start on the defensive, we'll have better odds of winning."

Adaki nodded and took a deep breath in and out. Tearan's cruel words from earlier echoed in his head.

Seeing her friend tense up, Aera leaned over to Adaki. "Don't take anything Tearan says seriously. He's a weasel-snake. He wants you to feel bad so he can have a better chance of winning."

Adaki stood up straighter and nodded. He had to stay confident. **Adaki smiled at his opponents.** "Two Sunray Academy teams in the finals. That's pretty cool!"

From the other side of the stage, Tearan grinned. "Let's put on a good show."

Moriko snickered. "Too bad this isn't a cooking competition. Or a math quiz. Or a cat-bat talent show . . ."

Aera narrowed her eyes at these comments.

"We heard rumors about your weird training," said Tearan.

Botan crossed his large arms. "Sifu Chuan's old age must be getting to her."

"That's so rude." Jiyung glared.

"We'd be more than happy to share what we've learned," said Adaki, ignoring their taunts.

Tearan chuckled. "Confident, aren't we, weak link?"

Then Headmaster Shion's voice boomed. "Three, two, one—" She struck the gong. **"BEGIN!"**

With the gong's vibrations still ringing in his ears, Adaki started firebending giant pillars toward the opposing team. Just as before, Team Adaki began on defense—giant sweeping moves that could push their opponents back. The problem was . . . Team Undefeated had chosen the same tactic.

Fire pillars and waves swept across the stage but canceled each other out. After a couple minutes of this, Team Adaki knew they'd have to change their approach, or they'd exhaust themselves with these large defensive moves.

"This isn't working!" said Aera, lowering her defenses.

"Let's charge 'em!" roared Tearan.

Team Undefeated dashed across the stage. To avoid getting pushed back, Team Adaki also ran toward them, so they all met at the middle.

A flurry of close-range firebending broke out. Sujun almost knocked Moriko off her feet with a fire spin attack.

"Whoa!" yelled Moriko, dodging just in time. "Where did that come from?"

"Perfected that in our cooking class." Sujun smirked and rushed forward to strike again.

Akito struck at Jiyung with fire pinwheels. Jiyung continued to dodge while jumping forward with her own fire fist strikes.

"Wait, aren't you that weird girl who started singing during the math exam?" Akito taunted.

"That's me!" said Jiyung cheerily. **"Consider this my encore!"** She took a deep breath in and released a giant fan of fire just like Chuan had taught her. Akito gasped and dropped to the floor to dodge the attack.

Aera, the smallest member of Team Adaki, faced off against Botan, the largest member of Team Undefeated. Botan towered over Aera and laughed. "It's like fighting against an ant!" He stomped, creating a ring of fire where his foot hit the ground.

But Aera was faster than Botan. She zipped behind her opponent and jumped, launching a kick at his back and causing him to stumble. **"It's going to be embarrassing for you to lose to an ant, then,"** she said with a smile. She struck at him with a fire whip—a more aggressive version of her ribbon technique.

Adaki and Tearan traded fire punches and kicks, each attack blocking the other. Adaki did his best to keep up, putting as much force as he could into each move. But the strength of Tearan's blows began to overwhelm him. He was being pushed farther and farther back across the arena.

"I can't keep this up . . ." said Adaki breathlessly.

He defended himself from another one of Tearan's fire punches.

Tearan swept a fire wave at Adaki, which he jumped over. "You're only here because your teammates didn't mess up like you did!" Tearan taunted.

Despite his exhaustion, Adaki held his head high. "Isn't that the point of a team? **We all carry each other."**

Tearan scoffed, charging his next attack. "Let's see your friends get you out of *this*!"

Tearan created a ring of flames around his body. He charged at Adaki **like a giant meteor!**

Chapter Fifteen

Adaki barely had time to react to the inferno hurtling toward him. He threw himself to the ground just in time to dodge his opponent. But Adaki's pants leg was set alight by the stray flames from Tearan's charge.

"GAH!" Adaki cried.

Still running, Tearan looked over his shoulder. He grinned when he saw Adaki rolling on the ground to put out his burning clothes. Tearan dug his heels into the ground to slow down, but **he was going so fast that he slid into Moriko,** who was locked in battle with Sujun. Moriko fell back onto the floor.

"Tearan?!" said Moriko, scrambling to her feet. "What the flying frog are you doing?!"

Tearan ignored her as he walked back toward Adaki.

Adaki, having extinguished his burning pants leg, stood up.

"HEY!" Moriko hurried after Tearan and shoved him from behind. "I'm talking to you! Why did you knock me over?!"

Tearan stumbled. He spun around, enraged. "It was an accident!" Tearan pushed her away. "Now back off, bozo! I've almost knocked out the runt!"

Sujun stood there awkwardly, looking between Moriko and Tearan. **"Um, are we gonna continue our fight, or . . . ?"**

Moriko was fuming. "Did you just call me *bozo*?!" she shrieked. In her rage, she threw a fire punch toward Tearan.

Caught off guard, Tearan instinctively blocked the attack with a powerful fire blast of his own.

Before anyone could help her, **Moriko was sent flying offstage.** She landed on a referee, who cushioned her fall.

The squashed referee declared a muffled **"OUT!"**

Adaki's jaw dropped, and he stared in disbelief. "What just happened . . . ?!"

Even Tearan was shocked. "Oops."

"WHO IS THE BOZO NOW, TEARAN?!" Moriko shouted from offstage.

Akito and Botan glanced over at Moriko, confused by the commotion.

Jiyung and Aera, who were midbattle with Akito and Botan, were too focused on the fight to notice. They both landed their attacks while their opponents were distracted. Jiyung's fire breath and Aera's fire whip knocked Akito and Botan out of bounds.

"OUT!" declared one referee.

"OUT!" shouted another.

Tearan snarled. "Blockheads, the lot of them!"

Adaki, Jiyung, Aera, and Sujun surrounded Tearan on the stage.

"I bet you think because there are four of you, you have the advantage now." Tearan smirked, his eye twitching. "Well, think again!" Tearan took a fighting stance, his clenched fists shrouded with flames. "I'll do worse than burn your pants next time, matchstick!"

"Tearan will do anything to win," said Jiyung to the team. **"We need to put an end to this quickly, before anybody gets hurt!"**

Aera looked up at where the lantern hung. "I think it might be time to capture the lantern. Keep Tearan busy and I can try for it!"

Sujun nodded. "Come on, let's end this thing!"

Team Adaki circled Tearan. Meanwhile, Aera created a fire ribbon.

Tearan rolled his eyes. "Could you be more obvious?" He ran toward Aera, his flaming fists thrust forward to split up the group surrounding him.

Aera moved the fire ribbon to strike Tearan like a whip, putting space between them. "Back off, blockhead!"

"He can't attack us all at once!" said Adaki. **"Let's go for the lantern at the same time!"**

Adaki, Jiyung, and Sujun ran to opposite ends of the stage and created fire ribbons of their own.

The audience *ooooohe*d at the sight.

Tearan spun around. "Oh no you don't . . ." He threw kicks and punches into the air, each generating a stream of fire.

But the ribbons of fire moved in unpredictable twirls and loops. **Tearan's attacks, while powerful, couldn't keep up.**

The ribbons all reached the lantern at the same time, and together, **Team Adaki cut the rope!**

As the paper lantern floated downward, Tearan stood at the center of the stage—directly below it. "Thanks for cutting it down for me!" He laughed.

Adaki, Jiyung, Sujun, and Aera ran toward Tearan. But he fended them off with fire stream blasts.

"It's no use. We can't get past him!" said Jiyung.

Adaki looked up at the lantern as it drifted downward. It gave him an idea . . .

"If the ribbons could get past him, so can we!"

Adaki dashed toward Tearan. He generated a small fireball and threw it at him. Tearan knocked the fireball away with ease.

"You really think such a weak move would work against me, matchstick?" mocked Tearan, sending a fire blast his way.

Adaki dodged the attack, then ran in a zigzag pattern. He rapidly hurled more small fireballs toward Tearan. Tearan staggered around as he tried to both deflect the rapid attacks and keep up with Adaki's unpredictable movements. But even with Tearan's powerful fire stream punches, he couldn't land a hit on Adaki.

Tearan glanced up, and the lantern was drifting closer. "Nice try, but I'm still going to win—"

But then he looked back down and discovered he had lost sight of Adaki, who had dashed behind him. Before Tearan realized what was happening, **Adaki nimbly climbed up his opponent's back, stood on his shoulders, launched himself upward . . .**

And caught the lantern!

Adaki landed on the ground and held it up in the air triumphantly. "We did it!"

The headmaster stood up and announced, **"THE VICTORY GOES TO TEAM ADAKI!"**

Adaki, Jiyung, Sujun, and Aera couldn't believe it! The audience erupted into cheers. Sifu Chuan cheered especially loudly.

Adaki's father made his way down from the stands and hurried to his son. "Adaki, **you were incredible!"** He embraced his son. "I could barely keep up with your speed!"

"Being a matchstick has its perks!" Adaki laughed, hugging his dad before pulling back and looking up at him with a big grin. "And now I can buy you a bigger boat!"

Adaro stared in shock, then shook his head. "No, Adaki, **this was your victory!** You need to treat *yourself* and your friends first of all . . . maybe to dinner!"

Adaki smiled widely as he looked over at his team. Jiyung's and Sujun's parents had come down from the stands to congratulate them, and Aera's grandma was giving her a big hug.

Headmaster Shion's voice boomed over the crowd. "Honored guests of the fourth annual Regional Bending Tournament, **please join me one more time in celebrating our winners: Jiyung, Sujun, Aera, and Adaki!"**

Chuan stood and cheered enthusiastically from the sidelines. "WAY TO GO, TEAM!"

Jiyung, Sujun, and Aera ran to Adaki's side. They all waved to Chuan.

"We couldn't have done this without you, Sifu!" called Adaki.

"Adaki, that last stunt you pulled was amazing!" said Jiyung.

"You moved just like a fire ribbon!" said Aera. "Buddy would be proud!"

"And using Tearan as a launchpad was awesome!" said Sujun.

They looked to the sidelines, where Tearan was being yelled at by the rest of his teammates.

Adaki grinned. "Actually, I thought of a new name for us . . . How about **Team Matchsticks?"**

The four friends laughed together.

Now Adaki knew what it was like to have his own incredible team . . .

And he couldn't wait to show the rest of the Fire Nation how much further they'd go!